LINCOLN THEN AND NOW

MAURICE B. HODSON

VOLUME 1

This book is dedicated to my parents

MAURICE AND NELLIE HODSON

to whom many of the old scenes illustrated here were
familiar sights during their childhood

Published by: M. B. Hodson, 30 Malton Road, North Hykeham, Lincoln. LN6 8HR
Printed by: Thorndyke Press Ltd., Corringham Road Industrial Estate, Gainsborough, Lincolnshire. DN21 1QB

FOREWORD

"The old order changeth, yielding place to new..."

Alfred Lord Tennyson

Tennyson, in a few words, stated an irrevocable principle though in quite a different context. Change is inevitable and one of the functions of the historian is to capture and record this process by various means. Some spend years carefully studying manuscripts - records of life and events down the centuries and by patient and critical assessment of recorded facts seek to set down their conclusions in writing, leaving the reader to build up a mental picture of place, events or society at that period. The account does, however, so often lack another dimension that would bring the whole scene to life. Hence the inclusion of pictures, diagrams, charts and other illustrations better to express the points made in the text. Others by the skilled use of line, colour and wash capture the detail of scene and period by recording some aspect of topography or family history that is a vivid reminder of their period. Atmosphere as well as detail can be conveyed through this flexible, sensitive medium but here again the artist may be tempted to enhance or omit critical points in the record. Always a matter of choice and interpretation.

There is an old saying "the camera never lies"! This is true only to a point for surprisingly the camera can sometimes fail to capture the detail that is so needed for a critical study. Record photography is a valuable aspect of local history studies. In this volume photographs of sights and scenes, often enlivened by fascinating people, recorded in many cases for the production of the ever-popular postcard, are set alongside the same view today recorded by high-quality modern cameras and techniques. What a splendid thing for the ardent collector of postcards and old photographs with all their nostalgia to team up with a friend who is an expert photographer and is prepared to place his camera on the identical spot today from which the old picture was recorded. A stark reminder of change and a dramatic illustration of Tennyson's old principle. What a change! How arresting to see local history portrayed in contrasting pictures in this way. What a valuable piece of work to have achieved.

Congratulations to Maurice Hodson and Peter Washbourn for this painstaking piece of local history record. It will be good to have supplementary volumes and a further series to update them in another 25/50 years!

F. T. BAKER

Chairman
Lincoln Civic Trust
November 1982

INTRODUCTION

My aim in publishing this book is to provide a visual comparison between present-day Lincoln and views of our city taken by photographers earlier this century.

It is in no way intended to give a balanced picture of the city between specific dates, but rather to show some of the changes that have taken place over the years.

Perhaps the most significant change in the city is in the area it now occupies when compared with, say, the period between the First and Second World Wars. Several large council housing estates have been built over the last fifty or so years, and the majority of the slum areas have been gradually eradicated, e.g. Stamp End and Waterside, the courts, yards and terraces of the old Drapery in Michaelgate, the land between Sincil Street and Melville Street, and the Great Northern Terrace area.

From St. Mark's in the north to Bracebridge in the south the River Witham effectively provided the western boundary of urban development and present-day Lincolnians must find it difficult to visualise this once sparsely populated area to the west of the Witham bereft of the Boultham, Hartsholme and Birchwood housing estates.

Equally, the fields to the north of the city on either side of the old Roman Ermine Street have been transformed into the St. Giles and Ermine housing estates.

The map on the inside of the back cover illustrates the extent of development that has taken place since 1920.

The great majority of the old views illustrated are from my own collection, and I gratefully acknowledge the help extended to me by the loan of material, etc. by various other people whose names appear below.

All the photographs of present-day Lincoln have been taken by Peter Washbourn, whose expertise and enthusiasm have proved invaluable and whose help I readily acknowledge.

The following people and organisations have kindly allowed their photographs to be copied and used in this publication or have given me valuable help and encouragement during the compilation of this book over the last eighteen months and to whom I extend my sincere thanks:

ACKNOWLEDGEMENTS

Richard Arden
Bill Baker
F.T. Baker, O.B.E., M.A.
C.A. Bridge
Mike Cobb
Eric Croft
James Dawson and Son Ltd.
Mr. and Mrs. J. Farnsworth
Maurice Ferrara
Geoffrey Fletcher
Leslie Hare
V. LeTall
Lincoln City Football Club Co. Ltd.
Lincolnshire Echo
S.T. Lucas, M.A.
C.V. Middleton and Son
N.B.S.
D. Peel
J.W. Ruddock
Henry Spencer and Sons
Don Teesdale
Peter Washbourn

SOURCES

1. The Local Studies Collection, Lincoln Library, by courtesy of Lincolnshire Library Service.
2. Elvin, L., *Lincoln As It Was.* Vols. 1-1V, 1974-1981. Hendon Publishing Company Limited

I would also like to thank my daughter Linda, who, in between travelling from one end of the country to the other in support of Lincoln City's "Red Imps", has managed to find the time to type the text.

Maurice B. Hodson. 1982

Silver Street, circa 1920, looking east. A much narrower Silver Street than now, with traffic flowing in both directions and not a yellow line in sight. Mansell's, watchmakers and jewellers, are on the corner of Flaxengate and the Lincoln Co-operative Society occupy the premises on the opposite side of the street. Note the old lamp standard a little beyond Mansell's.

Today, Silver Street is part of our "one way" traffic system. Mansell's and the Co-operative Society still occupy the same positions. The Co-operative Society's premises were demolished and rebuilt in 1961, only to be gutted by fire in 1965 and, after rebuilding, were again extensively damaged by yet another fire in 1969. The shops on the eastern corner of Free School Lane were demolished and rebuilt by the Co-operative Society in 1930. They are now derelict and due to be demolished or refurbished in 1983. Although the old decorative lamp standards were taken down many years ago, one can still be seen in the grounds of the Arboretum.

High Street, looking north - this interesting view is of High Street immediately to the north of the old Midland Crossing and illustrates the leisurely pace of life before the First World War. On left of picture the shop with the striped canopy is that of Boots, the chemists, who have been in the city since 1884. They also had another shop at the top of High Street. The spire of St. Mark's Church can be seen above Boots' shop. The stone building on right of picture is Sibthorp House, formerly the home of the family of the same name and who later moved to Canwick. The advertisement of Murfin's the grocers is prominently situated above their shop, which also served as St. Mark's Post Office at one time.

Today, Boots' old shop is now a leisure centre. St. Mark's Church was demolished in 1972 but the trees were allowed to stay, unlike Sibthorp House, which was, unfortunately, demolished in 1962. Shops and offices now occupy the site, which is still named Sibthorp House. Electric trams were withdrawn in 1929 and the tram lines were taken up shortly afterwards.

Celebrations in the city for the Coronation of King Edward V11 in 1901 included decoration of some of the archways. This photograph is of Newport Arch, formerly the northern gateway to the Roman City. The present arch was built circa 250 A.D. on the site of two earlier Roman gateways. The boys standing by the arch are wearing their Coronation medals presented by the schools. The lighting was by night-lights enclosed in small coloured glass jars suspended around the arch, across the top and on the crown.

The shop seen to the left of the archway has been demolished and the Co-operative Society built their new stores a few yards to the west in 1938. The lamp close to the postern gate has been removed and in recent years the Arch has been floodlit by night. Newport Cottage, seen on the east side of the gateway, appears almost unchanged in eighty years. To the right of Newport Cottage is East Bight, known as Tompitt Lane in the nineteenth century.

The Witham at Bracebridge, circa 1910. This pretty picture illustrates the tranquillity of life before the First World War. The steps on the left lead up to the Plough Inn from where the boats are hired. At this time the overhanging trees on the bank added charm to an already picturesque view of the winding Witham.

Today, sadly, the landing stage and steps are gone and the hiring of rowing boats from The Plough was discontinued many years ago. The banks on the east side of the river have been built up and strengthened as a precaution against flooding and some of the charm of earlier years has been lost by the removal of the overhanging trees.

Newland, 1907. Numerous post cards were published to commemorate the visit of King Edward V11 to The Royal Show, which was held on the West Common from 25th to 29th June, 1907. This illustration shows a gaily bedecked Newland, with many of the local residents in their finery, on their way to the Show.

Today, much evidence of the age of the motor car may be seen. On left of illustration is the Co-operative filling station, with a pedestrian crossing a little beyond. One wonders what the Edwardians would have thought of these strange yellow and white geometric signs in the road and the three striped ''totem poles'' with flashing heads!

Wests had occupied their High Street premises for about seven years when this fire took place on 6th August 1907. A little later they acquired the shop on the corner of Gaunt Street, then occupied by The Public Benefit Boot Co., and also the stone built house on right of picture, which was demolished and converted into show rooms for the sale of motor cars. Having moved into High Street from Canwick Road, the hairdressing side of the business was still carried on as indicated by the notice on the shop window, 'Haircut 3d' (fractionally more than one new penny today!). A crowd of interested bystanders watch the firemen's efforts to quell the blaze, completely blocking High Street in the process.

Now, after nearly 100 years of trading in the city, the West family are no longer associated with the Company and the premises are empty and for sale. At one time, West's also dealt in tractors and other agricultural machinery and employed approximately eighty people.

Newark Road, Bracebridge, circa 1920. In 1920 Newark Road, at this point crossing the Witham at Bracebridge, appeared to be a sleepy, wooded country lane. On the right can be seen the Plough Inn and the sign on the side of the building indicates that boats may be hired from this inn on the banks of the Witham. Further down the road is another inn, the Waggon and Horses. On the street lamp in right foreground a white painted section can be seen. This was a reminder from World War 1, when lamp posts and other encumbrances were so indicated for the safety of pedestrians after dark.

A sharp contrast in traffic conditions today on a much widened road and bridge which forms part of the A46 trunk road. The new bridge was constructed in 1925/26. Both the Plough and the Waggon and Horses are there today, but boats are no longer for hire from the former. Many of the trees were taken down during the road improvements and a garage occupies much of the land on left of picture. The buildings seen beyond the Waggon and Horses and situated at the junction of Newark Road and Rookery Lane are shops with living accommodation. They were built in 1960/61.

The Carholme, 1914. The military were in occupation of the stables and buildings at the racecourse during the First World War. Horse racing had been carried on at The Carholme since the 18th century and the famous and long established Lincolnshire Handicap was held in March of each year.

Racing 'on the flat' finished on The Carholme in 1964 when the governing authorities withdrew the levy. Sadly, the 'Handicap' is now run at Doncaster. Point to Point racing only is now held on this ancient race course and the magic of 'Race Week' for many enthusiasts has probably gone for ever. The building beyond the Grand Stand was demolished in 1966 and the mature tree on the green in front of the stables has been taken down and replaced by newly planted saplings. The stables have been re-built to modern standards.

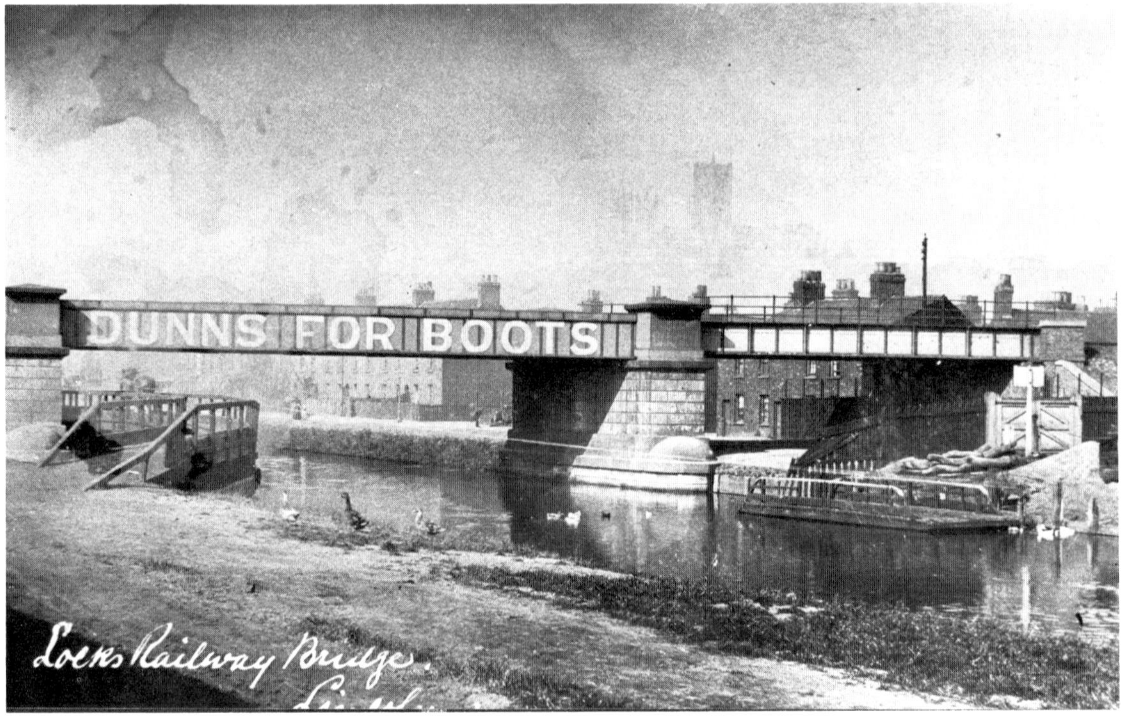

The Witham at Stamp End, circa 1908, looking north-west. The ducks in this scene help to create a pretty picture on what was normally a very busy river and roadway. Hundreds of workers employed at the world famous engineering firm of Clayton and Shuttleworth passed under the railway bridge daily and the strategically placed advertisement of Dunn's (whose shop was near to High Bridge) must have served as a constant reminder to them. Note the ferry moored on the north bank and also the wooden structure, on which a horse is being led, on the south bank. The horse is towing a barge which is just out of the picture. This bridge-like structure was built in order to allow the horses towing the barges to pass freely under the bridge and consequently no unharnessing of the horses was necessary.

Today Shuttleworth House blots out the view of the Cathedral. On the north bank, while some of the piers to the landing stage still remain, the ferry is no more. However, on the south bank, although the commercial river trade has now ceased, the wooden planked passing point for the barge horses is still there today, but is hidden by the small trees in this illustration. A retaining fence has been fixed to that part of the bridge spanning the river.

In 1910 Brayford was one of the busiest areas of the city and on the north and east wharves were mills, warehouses and other places of business connected with the thriving river trade. Barges from the Humber and Trent found their way into the busy inland port at Lincoln which was so near to the city centre. They came via the Fossdyke Canal, cut by the Romans nearly two thousand years ago, linking the Trent and Humber with one of their most important towns, *Lindum Colonia,* as it then was.

A different type of boat occupies the moorings today with the commercial river trade finished. Brayford and the Fossdyke are used mainly for recreational purposes and an annual water festival is held on Brayford Pool, attracting huge crowds. Many of the buildings around the Pool have been demolished and replaced by modern offices, car parks, etc. The removal of Brayford Head Bridge and the demolition of the old buildings, together with the construction of Wigford Way, has dramatically changed this 19th century waterfront.

This photograph of Alex Christopher, proudly standing with his new cart in front of Dickinson's Mill on Brayford Wharf East, was taken about 1925. A well known character in the city, Alex was a carting contractor and horse dealer, etc. He lived at the old Crown and Woolpack Inn situated in Brayford Street. In later years he was a familiar sight in the city streets in his pony and trap sporting his customary buttonhole. His popular slogan was "We lead others follow".

Melville Street, looking north, some years prior to the building of Pelham Bridge in 1957/58. Some of the property on the west side to the north of Norman Street has already been demolished.

The building of Pelham Bridge has transformed this rather narrow dingy stretch of Melville Street into probably the busiest route through the city. During the summer months the traffic is particularly heavy due to holiday makers aiming for the nearby coastal resorts of Skegness, Mablethorpe and Cleethorpes. The road curving away on right of picture leads under Pelham Bridge into Oxford Street. As a direct consequence of the traffic situation a footbridge has been built over the roadway, near to Thorn Bridge, and a more open aspect has been achieved by the demolition of the old shops and houses on the east side of the street.

This view, taken about 1910, shows Langworth Gate Post Office with the sub-postmaster, Frank Hardy, standing in the doorway of his shop with, possibly, his grand-daughter. These were the days of five deliveries of mail during the day, at 7.00 a.m., 10.30 a.m., 1.30 p.m., 4.30 p.m. and 7.30 p.m. and 'The General', in Guildhall Street, was open until 10.00 p.m. The Hardy family ran the post office from 1909 to about the mid 1930's. Mr. Hardy appears to have used the maximum space to advertise that he was also a newsagent. On one of his advertisements the price of Red Cut Virginia Tobacco is shown as four old pence per ounce!. The sign seen on left of building is that of John J. Coupland, plumber. Curiously, the official address of Langworth Gate Post Office was 22 Eastgate.

Last used as a post office in the mid-1930's, this building dating from the mid-18th century is basically unchanged, except for the acquisition of a bay window, TV aerial and a 'No Entry' sign. When this photograph was taken the old shop was still being used as a ladies hairdressing salon, but is now a private dwelling.

Prior to 1846 markets were held in various parts of the City; the Butter Market was a little to the north of the Stonebow, the Fish Market on High Bridge, at one time the Cloth Market was held in the 'Drapery' in the Michaelgate area and there was a general market in High Street between St. Mark's and High Bridge. In 1846 a public meeting was held and a resolution passed asking the Corporation to provide a permanent site for the City Markets on or near the Cornhill. This photograph, circa 1907, shows a busy Friday or Saturday market scene with the original Corn Exchange building immediately behind the market stalls. The building with the tower is a later and much bigger Corn Exchange built in 1879 and the New Market can be seen beyond the tall buildings on right of picture. Seventy-five years ago there were several pubs and hotels in the busy market area; on the Cornhill was the City Hotel and the Cornhill Hotel and in Sincil Street the Willow Pattern, Robin Hood, Newmarket and The New Bridge Inn. Other traders around the west end of the Cornhill were; brewers, gun and cycle makers, butchers, hosiers, corn merchants, confectioners, and tobacconists and hairdressers.

Most of the traditional character of this part of the market area disappeared when the stall holders lost their 'pitches' on the central cobbled area. Now the square has been pedestrianised with modern paving slabs and a small area devoted to plants and pleasantly flowering trees fronting on to High Street. The area behind the trees remains cobbled and seats have been provided for passers-by. Almost all of the small shops, together with the Cornhill Hotel and the City Hotel have gone and the south side of the square has been demolished and completely rebuilt and is now occupied by two building societies, two insurance companies and a bank, with yet two more building societies on the north side of the old open market area. Several of the buildings on the north side of the Cornhill remain, although somewhat altered, including the rather fine building next door to Melbourne Bros.. When this photograph was taken, the annual Wine Festival held each June, was in progress.

Above

Broadgate looking south, 1938. Once a familiar sight at the foot of Lindum Hill, the 'Bobby in the Tub' was replaced by automatic signals only in the '50's. In this photograph an experimental traffic island was in position and the 'Bobby's Tub' with overhead light was also in a temporary position. Shipley's, the ironmongers, can be seen on the corner of Unity Square with Houltby & Sons, grocers, a little lower down the street.

Below

After a fatal accident in 1971, when a lorry shed its load while coming out of Silver Street, the camber in the roadway was lessened and a wall was erected on the east side of Broadgate. As a result, the level of the pavement is below that of the roadway. As part of a redevelopment scheme both Shipley's and Houltby's have been demolished, with the former being incorporated into Jackson Shipley Limited, whose builders merchants premises, at the south end of Pelham Bridge, once formed part of Robey's works. The Post Office Telephone Exchange buildings now stand on the site of the old N.A.A.F.I. Club at the corner of St. Rumbold Street and in the distance can be seen the footbridge spanning Melville Street. On the west side of the street all the buildings between St. Swithin's Square and Thorngate have been demolished and redeveloped.

This photograph is of King EdwardVII driving down a gaily decorated Guildhall Street on his way to The Royal Show, which was held on the West Common between 25th and 29th June, 1907. In the early years of the century, cycling had become a very popular recreation and this is reflected by the sign seen outside The Raymond Hotel advertising 'Accommodation for Cyclists'. Some familiar names in Guildhall Street in 1907 included:- Walter Kirkham, hairdresser, R. W. Stokes, grocer, Miss A. Allott, baker and confectioner and Mowbray and Co. Ltd., brewers.

Today minimal structural alterations appear to have been made to the north side of Guildhall Street with the exception of the rather attractive building, formerly the Guildhall Hotel, to the east of The Raymond Hotel. This has been demolished and replaced by a modern structure occupied by one of the many building societies which have sprung up in the city centre almost overnight. The Raymond Hotel closed about 1910 and the Guildhall Hotel in 1907.

Waterside North, 1907. Clayton's A1 Fish and Oyster Saloon was situated on Waterside North, a little to the east of the Mayfield Bridge. This illustration shows a posed photograph of, presumably, the entire staff of the Fish and Oyster Saloon in 1907. During the years 1874-1890 the building served as the first home of Lincoln Liberal Club until it moved to new premises in St. Swithin's Square.

This 17th century building was superbly restored in 1979 by North Country Breweries and converted into The Witch and The Wardrobe pub.

In 1907 there were nine pubs on the riverside between High Bridge and Magpies Bridge (now Thorn Bridge). Today there is only The Witch and The Wardrobe and The Green Dragon, the latter now situated a little to the west of the original site in another magnificently restored 14th century house formerly known as 'The Great Garrettes'.

It was a "man's world" in 1907 when, in this scene, the Burton Hunt met in Eastgate at its junction with Langworth Gate and Greetwell Gate. Note the three young girls, probably domestic staff, looking with interest from the window at the colourful scene.

The Burton Hunt, already established by 1672, no longer meets in the city streets. Their final meeting in the city was held at Sobraon Barracks in 1973. The creeper clad walls of the nearby houses add a distinctive charm to the locality, especially in the autumn. The original stonework has been exposed on the upper section of the building on right of picture, further enhancing its appearance.

Magpies Bridge, circa 1905. In 1905 a much narrower bridge than we know today spanned the River Witham connecting Melville Street with Magpies Square. The Magpies Inn was established as early as 1791 and at the time this photograph was taken the posters on the building tell us that the property was for sale. The busy river trade must have provided much business for this riverside tavern, with, doubtless, many of the workers from the engineering works of Ruston and Proctor, and Clayton and Shuttleworth calling on their way home. The building on left of illustration is Kilmister's brushmakers and general warehousemen.

Demolished, rebuilt, widened and renamed in 1939/40 Magpies Bridge is now Thorn Bridge. The Magpies Inn closed before the First World War and later it was used as a dancing school, parish hall and restaurant. In the early 1920's the British Legion (now the Royal British Legion) moved from their club in Danes Terrace and bought the premises. The ornamental wrought iron railings of the earlier bridge contrast with a more functional type of ironwork which divides the dual carriageway from the foot of Pelham Bridge, almost to the automatic traffic signals situated at the bottom of Lindum Hill. The modern building beyond the Royal British Legion belongs to British Telecom and houses the automatic telephone exchange.

"The Saracens", as it was familiarly known, had been in High Street since at least 1496 and has been rebuilt on various occasions. Once one of the old coaching inns, it later became the largest hotel in the county with more than seventy bedrooms. Much of the hotel seen in this photograph was built on the court yard where the long distance stage coaches came in. At the turn of the century horse buses from the hotel attended the arrival and departure of all trains. From about 1935 the Saracen's Head, together with The White Hart in Bailgate, was owned by Lincoln Hotels Ltd., the major shareholder being Mr. H.H. Leven. In 1923 Mr. Leven acquired The Spread Eagle Hotel which adjoined "The Saracens". He promptly disposed of the property to Woolworth's, who had been seeking a suitable site in the city. "The Saracens" closed in 1959 to make way for more shops, much to the sorrow of many local residents. During the last war numerous servicemen stationed in the area spent many an enjoyable evening in the old and popular hotel. Mention of the Tudor Room, the Kitchener Room or the Beatty Room must bring back a host of memories to many an airman or soldier who served in the locality. Today, although the whole of the property has been converted into shops, the facade and wrought iron balcony have been retained and very little change is noticeable from the outside.

Top Left The Saracen's Head Hotel, 1959

Bottom Left The same view in 1982

Reception Area

Dining Room

SARACEN'S HEAD HOTEL
LINCOLN.

TELEPHONE 980 (3 LINES).
TELEGRAMS:
"SARACENS" LINCOLN.

Proprietor:
H. H. LEVEN.

ORDER OF LINCOLN HOTELS LTD

LINCOLN

Henry Spencer and Sons

ARE INSTRUCTED TO HOLD

An Important Four Days Sale by auction

OF

The Contents of

THE SARACEN'S HEAD HOTEL

AT THE HOTEL, ON

Tuesday, Wednesday, Thursday and Friday
8th, 9th, 10th and 11th December, 1959

INCLUDING

ANDSOME LOUNGE, DINING ROOM, BAR AND BANQUETING ROOM FURNITURE.

5 LEATHER AND UPHOLSTERED SINGLE CHAIRS (*suitable for Hotels and Confer-nce Rooms*). STUART OAK SETTLES. CHINESE ORNAMENTAL TEAK CHAIRS. A GREAT NUMBER OF DINING TABLES. SHERATON STYLE AND OTHER SIDEBOARDS AND SERVING TABLES. CHESTERFIELD SETTEES AND EASY HAIRS. ... MAHOGANY ...

This photograph of Priory Gate Arch was taken by Richard Marris early in 1905 after a heavy fall of snow. To the left of the archway is Eastgate House, then occupied by Alfred Shuttleworth, J.P., son of one of the founders of Clayton and Shuttleworth Limited, engineers. Almost hidden in the shadow of the archway can be seen a butcher's boy with his basket of meat, and another tradesman. The road surface under the arch suggests that gritting had just been carried out, possibly by the horse and cart seen at the junction of Eastgate and Northgate.

The same scene during the severe winter of 1981/82. Through the archway can be seen Eastgate Post House Hotel built in 1965 and to accommodate this modern building some of the property on Northgate has been demolished. Part of the old Eastgate House remains and is integrated into the new structure. On extreme left can just be seen the statue of Alfred Lord Tennyson, born in the county at Somersby in 1809 and Poet Laureate in 1850. The unveiling ceremony was on 15th July, 1905.

Portrayed in this photograph, taken in 1907, are some of the workers employed by Ruston and Proctor Limited (later Ruston and Hornsby) leaving work on Waterside South. This world-famous engineering company started life in 1840 as Burton and Proctor, millwrights. In 1857 the young and dynamic Joseph Ruston joined the firm and became the driving force behind what was to become a well respected and extremely successful company. In the last year of World War 1, Richard Hornsby & Sons Limited of Grantham was taken over and on 11th September 1918, Ruston and Hornsby Limited was born.

Today the building to the right, much altered, is a canteen. The mooring points for barges are still there, although unused, and safety chains have been fixed to the side of the canalised River Witham. Ruston and Hornsby was taken over by English Electric in 1961 and acquired by G.E.C. in 1966 and named Ruston Gas Turbines Ltd.

The Waterside, circa 1909, looking west. This photograph was probably taken from the Mayfield Bridge and among the hotchpotch of buildings on the north side can be seen in right foreground the corn mill of Henry Leetham & Sons. About this time, in the short distance between High Bridge and Mayfield Bridge, were the following pubs:- Lord Nelson Inn, Spread Eagle Vaults, Saracen's Head Tap, Labourer's Arms and Witham Inn. Opposite, on the south bank, was the Gardeners' Arms and long-forgotten addresses such as Kirton's Square, Straw's Court and Hewson's Passage. The obelisk can be seen on High Bridge, with Dunn's Boot Stores to the left.

Dramatic changes on both banks of the river since 1909 and more to follow, with the building of a new C & A Store on the south side in 1982/83. Woolworth's stores now occupy almost all of the north side and now there are no pubs on either side of this stretch of the river. On the south bank can be seen the new Montague Burton building with Marks & Spencer where once Dunn's Boot Stores stood near to High Bridge. Springtime brings a delightful aspect to this scene, with the trees in full bloom along the waterway and the City Council are to be complimented for providing such a charming view.

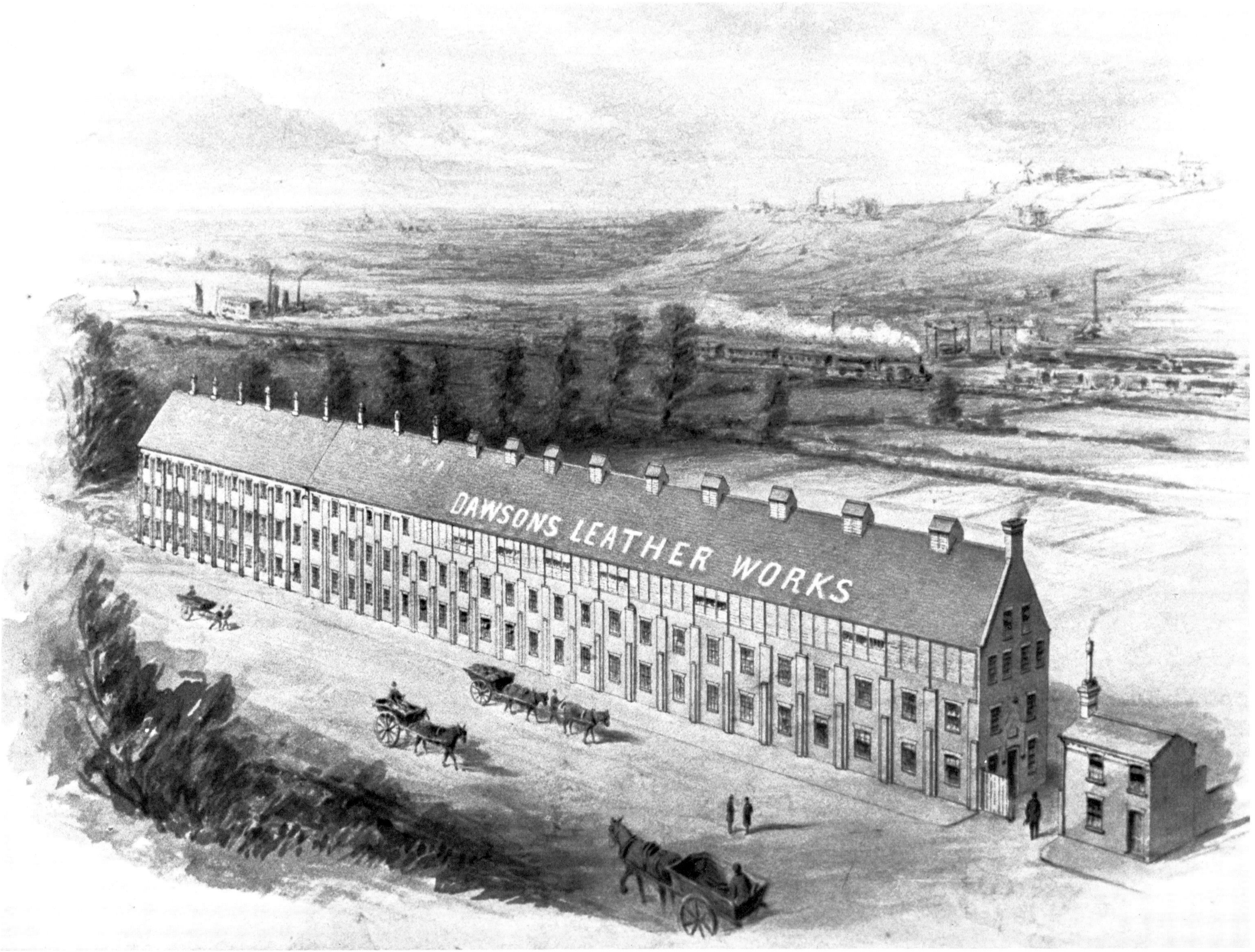
DAWSONS LEATHER WORKS

This illustration was taken around 1910 and shows the owner of this well kept pony and trap posing for the photographer outside Castle Hill House. Could this be one of the medical profession, who resided at the house about this time, setting off on his rounds?

Castle Hill House was, unfortunately, demolished in the late '30's and is now a car park. Much evidence of the age of the motor car is shown by the presence of double yellow lines on the road. The entrance to the castle has been greatly enhanced by the removal of the ivy over the gateway.

Left

Dawson's leather works, circa 1896. James Dawson was a bootmaker who came from Welton-by Lincoln in the 1870's. His first premises were situated in Sincil Street and he soon had two shops in the busy market area. By 1880 further expansion was needed and he moved his thriving leather belting business to a small works in Unity Square. These premises also became inadequate and his final move was to a new industrial estate at New Boultham - to land bought from Colonel Richard Ellison, of Boultham Hall. In this extremely interesting illustration, looking to the north-west, some of the windmills can be seen on the escarpment. To the left, sailing barges are just about to pass the fertiliser works of Jekyll, Glasier and Company (now Fisons Ltd.) on the Fossdyke and at the eastern end of Carholme Road two gasometers mark the site of the city's first gas works. The large house on upper right was then occupied by the Lincoln and Lincolnshire Home for Girls which in later yeas was the Lincolnshire Division Headquarters of the East Midlands Gas Board.

During the First World War a great part of the work was done for the War Office and this illustration is of the leather strapping department.

This photograph was taken in the early 1930's and shows some of the girls employed by Henry Poppleton and Sons decorating the various cakes and sweetmeats. Dawson's modern factory and ofice block now occupy the site.

The modern office block and factory shown in this picture stand on the site formerly occupied by Henry Poppleton and Sons, sweet manufacturers, whose premises were acquired by Dawson's in 1935. The partly demolished original factory is behind these buildings, but leather has long been outdated in the manufacture of belting for agriculture and industry. Dawson's are no longer a family business and they became a member of the Fenner Group, based at Hull, in 1978.

The Regal Cinema was proudly advertising ''Talkies'' when this photograph was taken in the early 1930's. Originally known as the Picture House when it opened in 1915, it also boasted a restaurant on the premises as indicated by the placard to the right of the entrance. Entry to the cheaper seats could be gained at the side entrance, situated down the quaintly named passage, Much Lane, which was between the Lincoln Waterproof Company shop and the Midland Bank.

The Regal, once one of seven cinemas in the city, closed in 1966 and was demolished, together with the premises formerly occupied by the family business of C. J. Fox Ltd., drapers, milliners, etc. since the last century, to make way for Littlewoods' stores. Trees and shrubs have been planted in this very busy area of the pedestrian precinct.

St. Paul's Church, Bailgate, was built in 1879 and demolished in 1971. It was the site of one of the earliest English churches believed to be built by order of Paulinus circa A.D. 627.

The same view today, with the church demolished and the trees rather dominating the still vacant site. A little of the Olde Worlde atmosphere remains, with the retention of the old gas lamp, now converted to electricity. After demolition archeological 'digs' were carried out on the site. The results are still being studied but evidence of a Saxon church was found and the pavements and walls of the Roman forum. The site will be displayed and made available for tourists in 1983.

South Park in 1957. This photograph was taken just before work started to divert South Park involving the construction of the new road, South Park Avenue. As can be seen in the illustration, traffic travelling along South Park had to negotiate the rather narrow bridge over the Lincoln/Grantham railway line. The road formerly ran parallel to the South Common in its entire length.

South Park and South Park Avenue today. South Park has been diverted and widened considerably and now follows a line a little to the north of the original road. The new section has been named South Park Avenue. A footpath connects the two stretches of the old South Park, drastically changing the eastern section overnight from a busy connecting road into a quiet backwater. Below the bridge the railway tracks were taken up after the line closed in 1965.

Richard Marris was a first class photographer, whose shop on Steep Hill was only a stone's throw from this part of Bailgate. When he took this photograph in 1907, Bailgate, or The Bail as many local residents know it, was a busy, bustling shopping area, as it is today. The horse drawn delivery van in right foreground had quite probably been making deliveries to such well remembered names as Holmes and Rosser, grocer and provision merchant and Seely's the grocer. Other familiar names included: F. P. Watson, chemist, Henry Kirke White, confectioner, William Elderkin, baker, John Maddison, butcher, and Albert George Dyke, cycle and motor manufacturer, who used the name R. M. Wright and Company as his trade name. St. Mary Magdalen church can be seen in the distance.

Today, Bailgate remains the most popular area for shoppers residing in the upper part of the city, despite parking restrictions. It is noteworthy that there have been very few structural alterations, after a period of more than 70 years. Watson's, chemist, are still in The Bail but Seely's, no longer a family grocery business, is now a restaurant. The Lion and Snake, Prince of Wales, White Hart Hotel and Duke William have all survived from 1907, unlike the following, which no longer exist:- Plough Hotel, Scarbrough Arms, Barley Mow Inn, Castle Tavern and Three Tuns Inn. The circle of stone setts in the roadway mark the site of the discovery of Roman columns in the 19th century.

High Street, looking north, circa 1924. On left of illustration can be seen the Great Northern Hotel and opposite is the goods receiving office for the same railway company, which was converted into the Great Northern Vaults. The hotel was one of the largest in the city until it was demolished in 1965. The signal seen immediately outside the goods office was for the benefit of the trams and not a railway signal. The electric trams were originally powered by studs in the roadway, but shortly after World War 1 the change to overhead power was made as the stud system was not entirely satisfactory. The cyclist in the picture appears to be quite oblivious of the following tram.

Today, the Great Northern Hotel and The Vaults have been replaced by modern buildings. At various times a supermarket and a furniture store occupied the site of the hotel and opposite a small block of shops have replaced the old Vaults.

This lively scene is of Saltergate in the mid 1920's, looking west. In right foreground is Battle & Co., wholesale druggists, who also had a long established shop on the corner of High Street and Silver Street. The building with the artificial stone facade is the old Corporation Offices, which extended northwards through to Silver Street. Farther along can be seen the Falcon Hotel, with the shop of Jacksons, cleaners and dyers, occupying the same prominent position that it does today.

Battle's wholesale warehouse was demolished in the 1940's and this section of Saltergate is now taken up by the Stonebow Centre — a tastefully designed and built shopping arcade which accommodates nine shops and provides a walk-through from Saltergate to Silver Street. Note how the window arches on the old buildings of Battle's and the Corporation Offices have been successfully reintroduced nearly sixty years later on the symmetrically designed ground floor of this modern shopping arcade. Even if this is co-incidental the effect is most pleasing.

The New Central Hall in St. Swithin's Square was built in 1902 to replace The Temperance Hall. The Central Hall was finally demolished in 1960 after a fire had completely gutted the interior in 1944. It was, surprisingly, allowed to remain and decay for 16 years, looking like an untidy reminder of bomb damage from the last war. The Central Hall continued its association with Temperance affairs but was also used as a concert hall and finally converted into the Central Cinema about 1920.

Thorngate House, the modern office block of Ruston Gas Turbines now occupies the site.

This photograph shows a Corporation bus passing under Pottergate Arch in the early 1930's. Lindum Hill (or New Road) was originally named Pottergate and the archway formed one of the entrances to the Cathedral Close. The road to the west of the arch was made in 1884.

Since 1938 Pottergate Arch has been closed to traffic and a road to the east of the gateway was constructed in the same year, enabling traffic to pass on either side in greater safety. The road sign on right of photograph indicates that heavy traffic is prohibited from travelling up Pottergate and past the Cathedral, as it has long been suspected that vibration from heavy vehicles is responsible for some of the damage to the fabric.

St. Mary's Street — 1925. Halford's cycle shop had occupied the corner of St. Mary's Street since 1910 and higher up the street was the Albion Hotel, which was also the home of the County Club. In the centre of the street can be seen the booking office for taxis. Hardly any street furniture and not a yellow line in sight.

Today, Halford's is still there, but completely rebuilt and extended. The Albion, once one of the city's best known hotels, no longer offers accommodation to visitors and the ground floor has been converted into a modern pub, now called the Barbican. The taxi booking office has been removed and, in the background, the Oxford Hotel has been incorporated into an enlarged and modernised Grand Hotel.

The line of property facing St. Mary's Street in this photograph, taken in the 1960's, was demolished in '70/71 to make way for Wigford Way. Prior to demolition some of the occupants were: W.J. Warrener & Sons, coal merchants, Lincoln Brick Co. Ltd., Chandler's Transport, Whitton and Ashley's Bar and, on the corner of Brayford Street, the long established business of Higgs Bros. tobacconists.

A dramatic change in the skyline with offices and a car park occupying prominent positions, but the level crossing is still just around the corner to the left!. Can there be a town in England of similar size, with level crossings only two hundred yards apart crossing the main street?. It remains to be seen what effect the removal of St. Mark's crossing will have in the future. The wall surrounding St. Mary-le-Wigford Church has gone as has one of the telephone boxes.

This photograph of the Durham Ox level crossing was taken just before work was started on the construction of Pelham Bridge in 1956.

The Durham Ox Hotel can be seen in centre of the illustration adjoining the garage of Gilbert and Son Ltd., with the works of Ruston and Hornsby Ltd., (formerly Newsum's timber works) on extreme right.

The building of Pelham Bridge was the largest and most important project undertaken in the city since the St. Swithin's Power Station was built in 1944.

Included in the 83 properties dispossessed in respect of the bridge scheme were 49 houses, 19 shops, 2 garages, 3 warehouses and a pub.

The locomotive passing over the crossing is a class J39 from the Lincoln sheds.

This locality has been dramatically transformed from a run-down late-Victorian neighbourhood, with the flow of road traffic continually held up by the closing of the level crossing, into a very busy modern fly-over, linked near to its southern end with South Park Avenue, which was constructed in 1960. Visitors to the city entering from the south and passing over Pelham Bridge are treated to an unsurpassed view of our magnificent Cathedral, as Ruskin wrote, "...the Cathedral at Lincoln is out and out the most precious piece of architecture in the British Isles, and roughly speaking, worth any two other Cathedrals we have got".

The bridge was opened for public use on December 10th, 1957 and the official opening ceremony was performed by Queen Elizabeth II when she visited the city on June 27th, 1958.

Despite protests from residents of Canwick Road and the Great Northern Terrace area, on grounds of inconvenience, the Durham Ox level crossing was finally closed on October 4th, 1959.

In addition to the modern bridge spanning the railway crossing, this photograph, taken in 1981, shows a radical change on the tracks below the bridge where diesel locomotives have replaced the old steam trains.

The Lincoln Arms, 114 High Street, circa 1900. This photograph shows one of the numerous Dawber & Co. owned pubs in the city. In addition to having in excess of 50 pubs they also had a brewery situated in Gas Street, off Carholme Road. Note the advertisement in the window for 'Hansom and Four Wheel Rubber Tyre Cabs for Hire'.

The Lincoln Arms today.

AND
PROVISION MERCHANTS
IN FAVOUR OVER
A QUARTER
OF A CENTURY

Left

This superb photograph of Francis Deakin and Son's Stamp End Bakery was taken around the turn of the century.

Established during the last quarter of the 19th century, Francis Deakin was not only a baker but also carried on business as a dealer in tea, grocer and provision merchant. His premises were situated near to Stamp End locks at 1 Alma Terrace, which was on the corner of Silverwood Place, with the Druids Arms opposite. He also had another shop in the west end of the city at 78 Carholme Road.

This posed photograph probably shows Mr. Deakin's children in addition to his bakery and delivery staff - and is that Mrs. Deakin peeping out of the bedroom window above the shop?.

The Stamp End Bakery was conveniently situated in the densely populated working class area of the industrial east end of the city and must have attracted a great deal of passing trade, both from the men who worked for the industrial giants Clayton and Shuttleworth, and Ruston and Proctor (later Ruston and Hornsby) as well as from the riverborne trade.

Mr. Deakin appears to have nearly as many items on display outside his shop as inside!. We can see sides of bacon hanging over his windows, with numerous hams above them, and on the floor we have the old-fashioned bread baskets with mountains of packaged soap etc. on either side.

Notice the hoist on the upper left of the photograph used for carrying bags of flour for the bakery and also the quaint two-wheeled doll's pushchair held by the young girl.

Right

The same view today from across the river, looking north, with the Stamp End locks in foreground.

Baggeholme Road, 1905. A typical scene during the harrowing days of the typhoid epidemic. In early 1905, the city was in the grip of a typhoid epidemic caused by a contaminated water supply. There were in excess of 1,000 notified cases and the death toll rose to 130. This photograph, taken at the junction of Baggeholme Road and Winn Street, shows local residents, equipped with various receptacles, awaiting the arrival of the water cart. Ironically, the collection point was the old water conduit erected in 1869 and situated in the centre of the road. The presence of the policeman has not deterred the boys from climbing the conduit. It is noticeable that in this photograph many of the younger people appear to be dressed in their 'Sunday Best'.

Since 1911 the city has obtained its water from Elkesley in Nottinghamshire, but the old water conduit was not removed until after World War Two. The houses on the south side of Winn Street were demolished about 1968 and replaced by Council flats which extend back to where the old Cannon Street used to be. This road junction and the surrounding area now has a much more open aspect than before.

Dixon Street, 1924, looking east. Opening up the Boultham estate from Dixon Street, this illustration shows the building of the bridge over the River Witham at Dixon Street nearly 60 years ago. A much smaller private bridge (shown below) spanned the river a few yards to the north of the present structure. This was dismantled and re-erected and now connects Russell Street, Bracebridge, with Boultham.

Dixon Street is an extremely busy thoroughfare today and is controlled by automatic traffic signals at both ends. Although the private bridge was taken down many years ago, part of the foundations can still be seen on the east bank of the Witham. The volume of traffic up and down the street today is so heavy that it has been found necessary to introduce parking restrictions, as indicated by the yellow lines on the bridge.

Newland, 1947. King George VI and Queen Elizabeth visited the city in 1947 on the occasion of the Royal Show, which was held on the West Common. To the right of the Swiss Cottage can be seen the shop formerly owned by Graves, Farnsworth & Co., for many years well known in the city as sweet manufacturers and confectioners. They also had shops at 6 The Strait, 277 and 396 High Street and a stall in the New Market. As they made their sweets on the premises it was always a delight for children - and adults too - to enter the shop and to smell the confections being made which including the enticing aromas of aniseed and mint, etc.. In addition to making all kinds of sweets, they are thought to have been the first makers of rock in the city and they also made their own ice cream. In this photograph, three generations of the Farnsworth family are to be seen crowding the first floor window and standing underneath the flag on right of the shop. The manufacturing side of the business ceased in the early years of World War Two and the premises were sold in 1958.

The same view today with the shop front almost unchanged, except for the attractive awning over the window. Ices are still sold, but are no longer made on the premises. Next door at the Swiss Cottage, and in line with modern eating and drinking habits, a sign indicates that snacks, etc., may be consumed on the premises. The tall concrete and glass building on extreme right of photograph is City Hall, built in 1973.

Canwick Road, 1907. Many of the houses in the St. Andrew's area of the city were built in the last century, like these on Canwick Road, primarily for the engineering workers of Robey and Co. Ltd., whose premises can just be seen on extreme right of picture. The grocer's shop on the corner of Cooling Street and Coultham Street was owned by Mr. F.W. Webb. The land behind the houses extending eastwards was bounded by the G.N. Railway to the north and the Cowpaddle and Robey's works to the south. Many of the men living in this area found employment working on the railway as engine drivers, porters, firemen, signalmen and plate layers, etc.. Although the consumption of alcohol by the working classes had only comparatively recently passed its peak, it is surprising that, in this predominantly working class area, there was only one pub. The Rose and Crown was situated in Dale Street and also provided changing rooms for the now defunct Lincoln Rovers F.C.. The 'corner shop' too was, curiously, almost non existent in this area, although there were a number of shops on Canwick Road between the Durham Ox level crossing and Great Northern Street.

The houses on Canwick Road were demolished by 1957 prior to the building of Pelham Bridge, together with some of the property then occupied by Robey's. Jackson Shipley Ltd., builders merchants, and a carpet warehouse now stand on land which was part of Robey's works and another new building, formerly a supermarket, is seen in left foreground. The Great Northern Terrace area was not demolished until about 1967/68 and is now an industrial estate. Several of the old street names have been retained, including Coultham Street, George Street and Cooling Street.

Ellis' Mill, Mill Road, circa 1910.

Lincoln's wind-swept escarpment once had a line of nine windmills. Six stood in Mill Road, with two more further along Burton Road (just beyond Yarborough Road) and one stood back in Mill Row. This important milling industry accepted the corn grown in the many open fields to the north of Lincoln. The last mill to survive was a tower-mill built in 1784. It worked until 1940 and had been operated in its last years by Mr. Frank Ellis and his father. It had its full complement of 4 sails until 1916 when two were removed owing to a weakness at the top of the mill. In 1977, Lincoln Civic Trust purchased the derelict tower, burnt out in 1973, and decided to restore it as a Queen's Jubilee Project. Today, the mill is in full working order and resplendent with four new sails. It attracts many visitors and produces excellent whole-meal flour.

Damaged by fire in 1973 - derelict in 1974

Purchased by Lincoln Civic Trust in 1977, restored, and opened in 1981.

St. Peter-at-Arches, Silver Street - 1921. The old Corporation church of St. Peter-at-Arches is to the left of this illustration and, although no longer there today, still gives its name to the locality. Adjoining it is the Butter Market. Note the advertisement on the bus for Jackson's, cleaners and dyers. On the south side of the street can be seen the Corporation Offices and a little beyond is the tall building housing the offices of the Royal Insurance Company.

St.-Peter-at-Arches Church was demolished in 1933 and the Butter Market shared the same fate in 1937. An impressive block of offices and shops now occupy the site. On the south side of the street the buildings of the Royal Insurance Company and the Co-op Society have been demolished and replaced by modern structures. The entrance to the Stonebow Centre, a shopping arcade built in 1981, connecting Silver Street with Saltergate, is now on the site where the Corporation Offices stood.

The stone lion in the Arboretum on Monks Road was presented in 1872 by F. J. Clarke, who was to have the honour of being four times Mayor of the City between 1878 and 1885. He lived at Bracebridge Hall and was the principal of a drug manufacturing company that sent its products all over the world. On 15th May 1909 the lion was defaced by having its face painted and by the addition of stripes as shown in the photograph. It was thought that some young apprentices were responsible but nothing was ever proved.

Today children on their first visit to the Arboretum are still taken to see the lion and it has remained a popular attraction over the last 110 years.

St. Andrew's Church and Infants' School, circa 1920. St. Andrew's Church was built in 1876/7 and demolished in 1970. When it was built, some of the fabric was obtained from old St. Martin's Church which was situated in St. Martin's Lane. The St. Andrew's area once formed part of the Parish of St. Peter-at-Gowts and the church was built in order to care for the spiritual needs of the inhabitants, many of whom were employed by Robey and Co. Ltd., situated on Canwick Road.

Today, the school is occupied by a firm of wholesale chemists and the bellcote has been removed. Additional buildings have been erected in front of the old school and the churchyard is now the car park. Fortunately, some of the trees that grew in the old churchyard have been allowed to remain and a small pond and rockery have been added. Now, with the church demolished, this district once again forms part of the St. Peter-at-Gowts parish.

Electric trams succeeded the horse-drawn trams in 1905 and in this photograph the first electric tram, gaily decorated and with civic dignitaries aboard, has stopped outside the Black Bull Hotel expressly for this photograph to be taken. The trams ran from St. Benedict Church in the north to the tram sheds at Bracebridge in the south. Patton's, pastry cooks and confectioners, can be seen next door to the Black Bull. Patton's also had tea rooms on the premises.

Yet another example of Lincoln's disappearing High Street hotels - the Black Bull closed in 1961 when British Home Stores premises were extended. The building to the right of the Black Bull remains, with its charming first floor windows contrasting sharply with its modern neighbour.

Boultham Park Road, early 1920's. When this photograph was taken Park Road, which was formerly part of the private driveway belonging to the Ellison family, was about to be developed. The drive started from a lodge on High Street (now Sharpe's Motor Cycles), crossed the Witham by a private bridge near to Dixon Street and ended in the well wooded park at Boultham Hall. The men seen in the background form part of the road-making gang.

The Boultham area has been transformed from a sparsely populated hamlet in the early 1920's into what is now the largest parish in the city, with a population of about twelve thousand. In the late 19th century the Ellison family started to dispose of the estate and a new industrial development was created in the northern corner, in the area which was to become New Boultham. Before the turn of the century James Dawson, a boot maker from Welton-by-Lincoln, had established a leather belting factory and next to him Henry Poppleton, a name familiar to many older residents, built a sweet factory on the corner of Beevor Street and the Ropewalk. Other well-known names, some to become world famous, acquired plots of land:- Ruston and Proctor Ltd. (later Ruston and Hornsby), William Foster and Co. Ltd., inventors of the tank in the First World War, and Cannon's, glue manufacturers. Today, New Boultham has become old Boultham and most of the houses, originally built to accommodate the labour force needed for industry, demolished. Ruston and Hornsby now form part of G.E.C. and Ruston-Bucyrus, an offshoot of Ruston and Hornsby, is also partly G.E.C.-owned. Foster's were taken over and closed a few years later and their premises were acquired by Ruston-Bucyrus Ltd. Cannon's glue factory was also closed and the site is now occupied by the G.E.C.-owned Ruston Gas Turbines Ltd. Dawson's had acquired Poppleton's factory in the aftermath of the depression in the 1930's. Boultham today is mainly residential and has both private dwellings and council housing estates.

Looking up Michaelgate from Hungate. This view was taken circa 1905. Michaelgate was part of the old Drapery area many years ago - the site of the cloth market. The Rising Sun Inn can be seen at the foot of the hill. Nearly all the old courts, yards, etc. off Michaelgate are long gone, including Woodhall's Yard, Shipley's Yard and the curiously named Birdcage Walk.

Today there are no cottages on the west side of Michaelgate and it has been left an untidy, overgrown hotchpotch of brick and stone. There has also been much demolition of the buildings on the opposite side of the street, including that of The Rising Sun, which is now a car park. The Harlequin Gallery situated at the top of the hill was a pub in 1905 and dates from the 16th century.

Monks Road - the old fairground and cattle market. The April Pleasure Fair was held on land now occupied by Lincoln College of Technology from the late 19th century until it was transferred to the South Common during the Second World War. An additional fair, held in August, was introduced about the same time, to augment the war time 'holidays at home' scheme. After the war the extra fair was retained and is now known as the Autumn Fair. The illustrations show the great popularity of the fair at the beginning of the century compared with the present day and its host of counter attractions. Fronting onto Monks Road are the pens of the cattle market, which closed in 1968.

The Cattle Market, circa 1920

Lincoln College of Technology, 1982

At first glance this would appear to be a photograph of the footbridge spanning the tracks at the Durham Ox level crossing. A closer inspection, however, will reveal the absence of steps at either end of the bridge. It is thought this photograph was taken before 1900 and is, in fact, a rodding bridge or gantry, whereby changing of the points at this junction was made by the signalman, from the signal box on left of illustration, activating the rods carried by the bridge. Between the signal box and the bridge can be seen the hostel used by railwaymen staying in the city overnight. Note the footbridge connecting Kesteven Street with Sincil Bank can just be seen in the distance.

More than eighty years later the rodding bridge has gone and the track is now spanned by Pelham Bridge, a modern fly-over opened by Queen Elizabeth II in 1958. The old cast-iron footbridge connecting Kesteven Street with Sincil Bank has been taken down and replaced by a modern structure. The railway hostel has also been demolished. Nowadays the rods controlling the points at this junction are laid underneath the track. The two sets of tracks are now interconnected enabling trains from the Central Station to run on the former Great Central lines to Market Rasen, Grimsby and Cleethorpes.

High Street looking south - early 1920's. On right of picture is the Great Northern Hotel, which was opened in 1848. Opposite can just be seen the stable block of the hotel, part of which was converted into the Great Northern Vaults. The spire of St. Mark's Church is in centre of picture with the trees in the churchyard producing a pleasant contrast with the surrounding buildings. It can be seen that the spire of St. Mark's Church is receiving attention at this time.

The Great Northern Hotel was demolished in 1965 to make way for yet more shops and two years later the Vaults shared the same fate. The criss-crossed area in the immediate foreground is now one of the busiest junctions in the city with Wigford Way, constructed in 1970, curving away to the right. St. Mark's Church was demolished in 1972.

Brayford, 1920's, looking north. All the property seen in this illustration on Brayford Wharf North has been demolished with the exception of the pub, Royal William IV. On extreme right the church tower of St. Peter-at-Arches (demolished in 1933) can just be seen.

The recently opened Sainsbury's stores has replaced some of the old buildings and a multi-storey car park occupies the site west of Sainsbury's, just off the picture. Across Wigford Way can be seen Littlewood's stores.

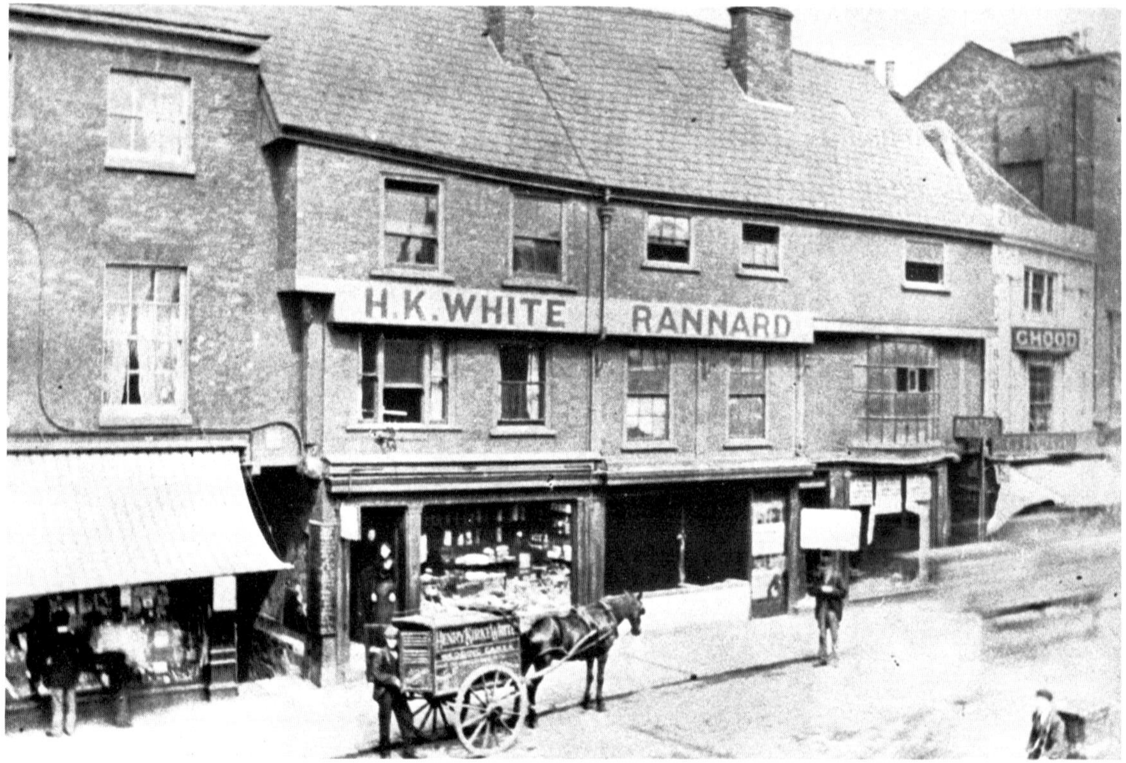

Almost unrecognisable as the west side of High Bridge, this photograph was taken in 1901, just before work started on the restoration of this 16th century house built on the bridge. High Bridge is unique in that it is the only mediaeval bridge in all England on which houses still stand. The horse drawn van is outside the baker's and confectioner's shop of Henry Kirke White, who also owned the Lindum Restaurant situated lower down High Street at the corner of Brayford Street. He also had other shops in the city, situated on Monks Road, Bailgate, Burton Road and High Street. The passage adjoining his shop in the photograph led down to South Witham Bank, where five cottages were tucked away from the busy city centre. The shops to the north of his premises appear to be unoccupied and the notices in the windows advise the public of the owners' new addresses. Rannard's were butchers and next door were Freshney's, milliners and drapers. Hood's boot stores can also be seen.

How superbly the Lincoln Corporation restored this 16th century house in 1902. Of great historical and architectural interest, it is an outstanding tourist attraction in the lower part of the city. Shops still occupy the ground floor but the upper floors are used by R. W. Stokes and Sons Limited as a restaurant and patrons partaking of a meal may also enjoy a delightful view of the Witham, particularly in the spring. Stokes', successors to Henry Kirke White, also have their well known coffee shop on the bridge and the enticing aroma of coffee beans attracts many a passer by. On each side of the building, steps still lead down to the river, but the cottages on both banks have long gone. Interestingly, not only are the years during which restoration took place indicated on the front of the house, but the names of the mayors, C.W. Pennell and J.W. Ruddock, are also shown

LINCOLN CITY FOOTBALL CLUB, 1904-5. PHOTO BY CALEB SMITH, LINCOLN

J. W. Giles, director. D. Calderhead, secretary, C. Laverick, G. Buist, W. Pallister, T. Waterson, trainer.
F. Quincey, director, E. Bentley, groundsman, G. Frazer, W. Simpson. P. Blow.
E. H. Brown, D. O'Donnell, J. Martin, M. O'Donnell, W. Watson.

Lincoln City F.C. were members of the Football League Division Two in 1904/5. They had played at Sincil Bank only since 1893, having moved from their former ground in the Sibthorp Street area, which was called John O'Gaunt's. The main entrance was through the Norman doorway of St. Mary's Guildhall (wrongly known as John O'Gaunt's stables). In rather illustrious company by today's playing standards, the City finished in ninth position, with Doncaster Rovers creating a record which still stands today by finishing bottom of the league with only 8 points! Winners were Liverpool with 58 points, runners-up were Bolton Wanderers and Manchester United were third. It may surprise modern football fans to learn that in sixth place were Gainsborough Trinity!

LINCOLN CITY FOOTBALL CLUB 1982-3

From left to right:-
Back Row:- David Beavon, Stuart Hibberd, Steve Thompson, Stuart Naylor, Tony Cunningham, David Felgate, Trevor Peake, Glenn Cockerill, Gordon Hobson.

Middle Row:- John Pickering (assistant manager), George Shipley, David Carr, Colin Murphy (manager), Phil Turner, Derek Bell, Bert Loxley (physio).

Front Row:- Paul Jones, Robert Riviere, Paul Brown, Chris Moyses, Gary Strodder.

The 'Red Imps' won promotion from Division IV in 1980/81 with Manager Colin Murphy at the helm and came within a hair's breadth of gaining promotion in successive seasons when they failed by only one point. A traumatic start to the 1982-3 season was made when, faced with a serious financial crisis, the directors asked the Lincoln City Council to buy the Sincil Bank Ground in order that the Club might remain solvent. The Council agreed to buy the ground for approximately £225,000 and leased it back to Lincoln City F.C. with an option to re-purchase. In spite of these difficulties and a much depleted playing staff, at the time of going to press the 'Red Imps' are at the top of Division III, having been in this position for ten weeks. Hopefully, they can maintain this form until the end of the season.

HANNAH MEMORIAL WESLEYAN CHAPEL, LINCOLN.

The Hannah Memorial Wesleyan Chapel was situated on the corner of Chaplin Street and High Street. Its imposing front was in the Italian classic character comprising a semi-detached portico of six Corinthian columns surmounted by cornice and pediment with wings on either side. The foundation stones were laid in 1873 and the building was finished in 1874 - it was finally opened on January 14th, 1875 in front of a congregation of 1,800 people. It cost approximately £5,000 to build.

The Hannah Memorial Chapel closed in 1962 and the congregation moved across the road to Portland Place (now Central Methodist). It was replaced in 1972 by the new Thomas Cooper Memorial Chapel whose old building was formally in St. Benedict Square until it was demolished to make way for extensions to Marks and Spencers. This new Chapel is completely out of character and some would say an ugly building. Thankfully it stands well back from the original building line - the trustees paid £150,000 for its erection. One wonders what the reply might have been if the same question as shown on the postcard featuring Hannah Memorial were to be asked of the new building!

A Century of Public Transport in the City

Although some of the larger hotels in the city, such as the Saracen's Head, White Hart and Spread Eagle, had their own horse buses which attended the arrival of all trains, it was not until the early 1880's that an organised horse bus service was in operation.

Jackson and Son ran horse-drawn buses between the city centre and Bracebridge until 1882 when Lincoln Tramways Co. was formed and a track was laid between the Gatehouse Hotel in Bracebridge and St. Benedict Square. The trams were horse-drawn and the journey took 20 minutes.

In 1904 Lincoln Corporation bought the privately owned Lincoln Tramways Co., and the next year the old horse-drawn trams were withdrawn from service and the new, but rather modest, electric tramway was opened on November 23rd 1905. The electric 'cars' also used the same route as the horse-powered vehicles and at one time there were plans to extend the service both to the east and to the west via Saltergate and Guildhall Street respectively. However, as indicated elsewhere in this publication, no action was taken.

Originally the system used by the electric trams involved metal studs set in the roadway, but this method did not prove entirely satisfactory and in 1919 the change to overhead power was adopted.

In the next year the first motor buses were purchased, and this heralded the beginning of the end of the "old faithfull" electric trams. The last tram ran on March 4th, 1929.

To quote Abell and Chambers in *The Story of Lincoln:* "In 1929 the motor bus took its place, and the jangle of the tram - the most nerve shattering noise, perhaps, ever heard in the long history of Lincoln streets - was heard no more."

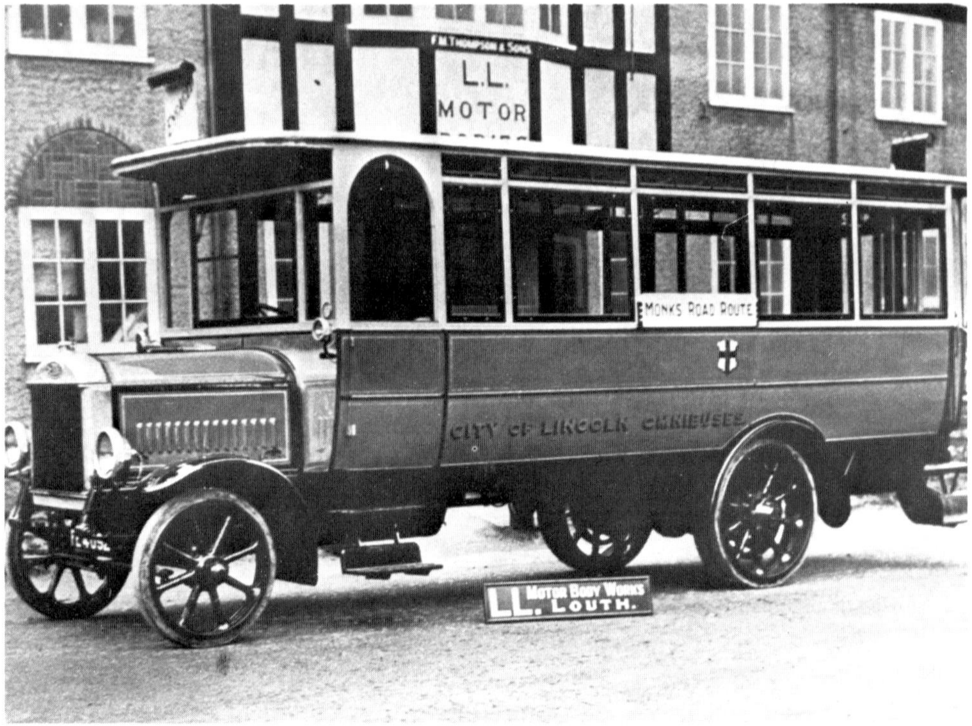

Top Left

One of Lincoln's first buses - a Dennis C.A.B. 1920/21. Photograph shows vehicle on display outside Coachbuilders premises in Louth.

Bottom Left

Leyland Titan T.D.1 1929

Above

A Bristol VRT decorated for the Royal Wedding in 1981.

Newark Road, Bracebridge, 1906, looking east. In centre of picture is the picturesque south lodge to Bracebridge Hall. The fountain in the centre of the road, for many years a well-known bus stop, was donated by the Rev. C. C. Ellison, vicar of Bracebridge and rector of Boultham from 1874 to 1911. He was brother to Colonel Sir Richard Ellison of Boultham Hall.

Seventy-five years later, the lodge is still with us and is now owned by the City Council. The fountain was dismantled about 1969 and the roadway is now much wider. With the removal of some of the trees, Brant Road (formerly Broughton Road) has been opened up and transformed from a sleepy country lane to a busy highway leading to several recently developed housing estates. The railings on the left of the illustration above have been removed and set back a little beyond the pathway constructed a few years earlier. This section of the road has been greatly improved and now allows pedestrians to walk in safety along the tree-lined pathway.

The Avenue, 1906. The dictionary defines an avenue as 'a roadway or approach bordered by regularly spaced trees' and so The Avenue was in 1906. A very much narrower approach to Yarborough Road than is the case today, with the overhanging trees meeting across the road.

Today much of the charm has been lost by the very necessary removal of all the trees and consequently the road has been appreciably widened to accommodate the heavy flow of traffic. Automatic traffic signals are in operation at its junction with West Parade.

Rookery Lane, formerly Boultham Lane, looking towards the city, circa 1914. Once part of the Boultham estate, Rookery Lane was not taken into the city boundary until 1920. Prior to 1950 the electorate voted in the Grantham division in parliamentary elections. The area is still known to older residents as Simon's Hill. This name probably originates from a favourite Ellison horse, in whose memory a monument (below) still stands nearby.

A far cry from a country lane before the First World War, Rookery Lane today is a very busy link road, connecting with the A46 to Newark and the southwest. Who would have thought that automatic traffic signals would be required at the end of this former country lane?

This view of High Street, looking south, early this century, shows an extremely busy main street with much horse traffic. The recently built Capital and Counties Bank (now Lloyds) stands proudly on the corner of St.Benedict Square, with Fowler's, coffee roasters, on the opposite corner. On left of picture can be seen the Black Goats Inn - later the Hotel Central. What appears to be a baker's delivery boy, carrying his wares on his head, walks down the centre of the street. Some of the market stalls on the Cornhill can just be seen.

In 1982 most of the buildings on the east side of the street have been demolished and rebuilt. Yet another hotel has gone - the Hotel Central closed about 1945 and Burton Menswear now occupies the site. Boots, the chemists, closed both of their shops in High Street and their new premises, soon to be extended, are opposite Lloyds Bank. Hepworth's, gents' outfitters, have been on the corner of the Cornhill since 1893. Barclays Bank can be seen on the other corner, with the tower of St. Mary-le-Wigford Church showing above. The cupola has been removed from what is now Lloyds Bank. The upper storeys of Dolcis shoe-shop are fine examples of Victorian architecture and survived a severe fire in 1977.

Saltergate looking west, circa 1900. The southern side of Saltergate was demolished in 1902 in order to afford access to vehicular traffic. In right foreground can be seen The Falcon Hotel, established circa 1791 and in left foreground is The Still, which was then owned by the well-known Pratt family. This cobbled, narrow and rather dingy alleyway, which was situated only a few yards from the heart of the city, is a typical example of Victorian urban development. As late as 1797 William Clayton was found guilty at Lincoln Assizes of stealing one silver pint mug and two silver half-pints, the property of Robert Ford, of the Falcon Inn, and was sentenced to death.

More than eighty years later, a much wider and cleaner Saltergate contrasts sharply with the narrow, ill-lit alley of the last century. Again, there is much evidence of the age of the motor car and double yellow lines and "No Entry" signs can be seen. Ironically, there has been no access to High Street from Saltergate for vehicular traffic for about thirty-five years and today the area both to the north and to the south of the Stonebow is pedestrianised. The Falcon is still there but is no longer an hotel and opposite is The Still, recently refurbished and modernised, but no longer owned by the Pratt family. On the north side of the street the building jutting out beyond The Falcon Inn is still occupied by Jacksons, cleaners and dyers in the city since 1840. The domed building on the corner of Guildhall Street is the Midland Bank, the site being occupied by Hepworths, gents' outfitters, until 1893.

The Diocesan School, Newport, 1907. Originally named The Diocesan School when it was built in 1842, its ultimate aim was to provide facilities for the training of village school teachers. However, this was not attained until twenty years later when, in 1862, it was renamed The Lincoln Diocesan Training College or The Training School for Mistresses and in that year student teachers were admitted.

The same view today from the south. The modern building hiding the original school was erected in 1971 and is the Sibthorp Library. It was provided by the benefaction of the late Mrs. Dudley Pelham (nee Sibthorp) of Canwick. In 1962 another change of name occurred when it became Bishop Grosseteste College, one of fourteen Church of England Colleges of Higher Education and a constituent college of Nottingham University. It takes its name from Robert Grosseteste, the mediaeval scientist, educator and Bishop of Lincoln from 1235 to 1254. Today the annual intake is approximately 120 students with men taking about 25 per cent of the places.

Some of the domestic staff circa 1924. Hours were long and discipline was keen in 1924 and the domestic staff were expected to attend morning service daily.

Starting work at 6.00 a.m., with some free time after lunch and dinner, work continued until 8.30 p.m. each day with one afternoon and evening off.

Wages were 8 shillings (40p) per week with meals and accommodation provided.

Thorn Bridge, 1949. The old Green Dragon Inn was for many years on the corner of Magpies Square and Waterside North. A little to the north can be seen the sale rooms of Pearson and Sindell, auctioneers. Some years earlier Choice's, pawnbrokers, had one of their shops on the corner of St. Swithin's Square. St. Swithin's Church can just be seen above the Green Dragon and the 14th century house adjoining it.

Dramatic changes today, with all the property completely demolished from the Waterside to St. Swithin's Square. The 14th century house has been splendidly restored and is now The Green Dragon Inn, with the modern office block of Ruston Gas Turbines adjacent. As a result of the demolition and rebuilding the east end of St. Swithin's Church is now visible from the bridge. The little used and controversially situated footbridge spanning the roadway provides an excellent view of the Cathedral for photographers.

This view of High Street was taken circa 1908 and shows quite clearly the studs between the tram lines which powered the electric trams. The upper deck of the tram cars was open to the weather until about 1910 when additional cars were purchased complete with enclosed upper decks. Although the change from surface powered studs to overhead power was made as late as 1919, with the resultant installation of numerous poles along High Street and Newark Road, the death knell of the trams was sounded shortly afterwards when, in 1920, the first motor buses were to be seen on the city streets. The trams lingered on until the last journey was made on 4th March 1929. As mentioned elsewhere in this publication, it is rather surprising to find that, during the years the electric tramways were in operation, 1905 to 1929, although various schemes were considered, no expansion of this rather modest system was ever implemented, and the trams continued to ply between St. Benedict Church and the Gatehouse Hotel, Bracebridge.

A vastly changed High Street today, with several new buildings to be seen. Barclays Bank has been demolished and rebuilt but the Black Swan remains and is now a shop. Boots' new premises can be seen on right of picture but the obelisk, formerly on High Bridge, was dismantled in 1939. The premises in left foreground, once used as a bank and restaurant, is now East Midlands Electricity Showrooms. The Queen Hotel, seen in right foreground, no longer offers accommodation and is now used as a restaurant. With the removal of the cupola from Lloyds Bank it is not quite the landmark it once was. This section of High Street was pedestrianised in 1974.

Top of High Street, early 1900's. On right of picture is the church of St. Peter-at-Arches, next to the old Butter Market. A little higher up the street can be seen the Blue Boar Inn. To the left is Beaumont's, grocers, later in business in Silver Street, with Harston's music shop next door. Beyond Harston's is Bainbridge's stores, established in the city since the middle of the last century. The cab rank was in front of St. Peter-at-Arches and is seen in the photograph.

St. Giles Church, today.

This area now forms part of the pedestrian precinct and is barely recognisable from earlier days. The old Butter Market and St. Peter-at-Arches Church were demolished in the '30's. Part of the fabric of both buildings were, coincidently, later incorporated into newer structures. The facade of the Butter Market now forms part of the Central Market on Waterside South and some of the fabric of the Church was used in the construction of St. Giles Church. The Blue Boar Inn closed about 1930. Opposite, the premises occupied by Beaumont's and Harston's were acquired by Mawer and Collingham's, until they, too, were taken over by the Fraser Group and renamed Binns.

Castle Hill, 1905. Another excellent photograph by local photographer Richard Marris, whose shop was nearby. Marris captures life in the early years of the century in this animated scene taken on Castle Hill. In 1905 the Assize Courts were held four times each year and the judges attended morning service at the Cathedral on the Sunday before the Courts were in session. No less than twelve policemen are in attendance as the coachman prepares to depart from the Judges' Lodgings, across the cobbled Castle Hill and through Exchequer Gate to the nearby Cathedral. The ivy-covered Castle Hill House may be seen on left of picture.

Nearly eighty years later the same scene is still enacted. In this photograph the judges, accompanied by court officials and escorted by a senior member of the Lincolnshire Constabulary are to be seen walking to the Cathedral for morning service. This traditional ceremony no longer appears to attract the interested crowd of onlookers as in earlier years. Today a car park stands on the site of Castle Hill House and the lamp in the centre of the still cobbled square has gone. The clinging ivy has been removed from over the entrance to the Castle.

C. J. FOX & CO., High-Class Gentleman's Tailors & Outfitters, 302, HIGH ST., LINCOLN.

The family business of C. J. Fox and Co., gentlemen's tailors and outfitters, were the occupants of 302 High Street in 1907. They also had a millinery and drapery shop almost opposite at number 216, next to the Regal Cinema.

Woolworth's commenced trading in the city almost sixty years ago when The Spread Eagle Hotel was acquired in 1923. The shop formerly occupied by C. J. Fox and Co. and later by Manfield and Sons Ltd., boot and shoe makers, was absorbed by Woolworth's about 1938 and Fox's remaining shop shared a similar fate in 1966, when it was bought by Littlewoods' stores and demolished, together with the adjoining property.

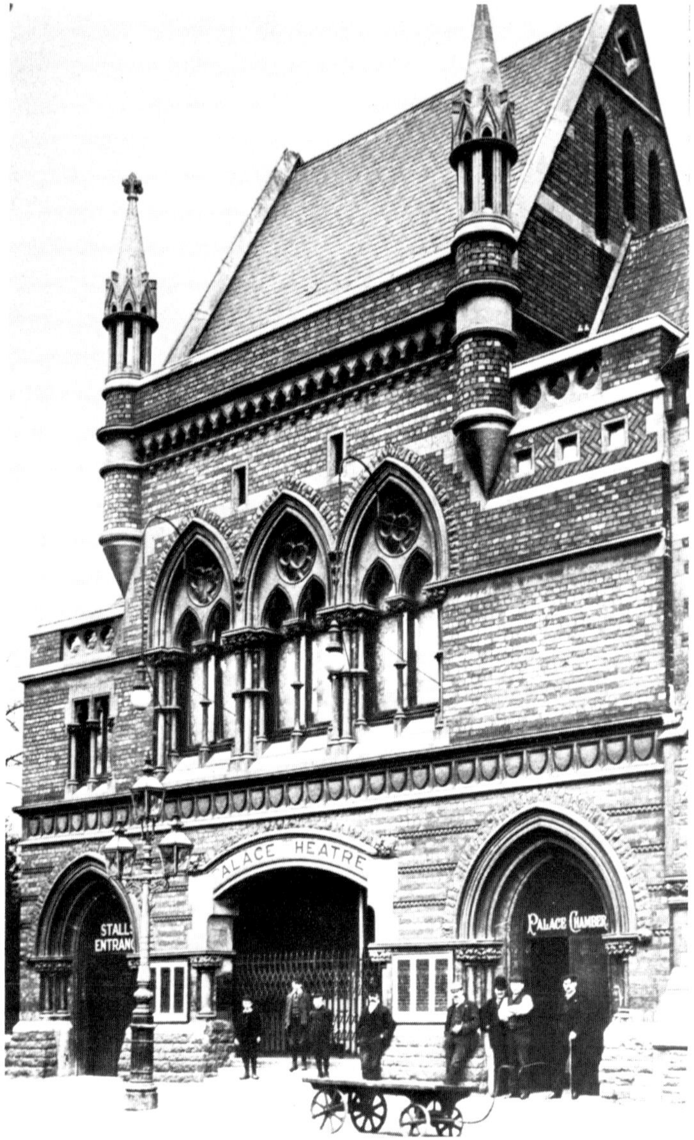

This view is of The Palace Theatre, Newland, circa 1910. Originally built as a masonic hall in 1872, it was converted into a music hall in the first year of this century and known as The Empire Theatre of Varieties. A change in ownership the very next year resulted in a change of name to The Palace Theatre. Yet another change of name occurred in 1931, when live shows were discontinued, and it re-opened as The Plaza Cinema. It was destroyed by fire in 1943.

The offices of the cumberously named National Employers' Mutual General Insurance Association Limited now stand on the site in this rather neat brick-built building which blends in so well with its surroundings.

This photograph of Magpies Square and Broadgate, circa late 1940's, taken from Thorn Bridge, provides a superb view of the Cathedral from the south. The shop on the corner of St. Swithin's Square is Choice's, the pawnbrokers, with Pearson and Sindell's Broadgate Salerooms next door. Spencer's, leather merchants and boot and shoe repairers, are at numbers 2/3, with the old Green Dragon on the corner of Waterside North. A little higher up in Broadgate, the premises immediately to the south of the Drill Hall are occupied by Parke, White and Arnold, mineral water manufacturers. The British Legion local club is in premises in immediate right foreground with G.R. James, undertakers, adjacent.

Now all the property on the west side of Magpies Square has been demolished and redeveloped with the new buildings set back, giving a more open aspect and also allowing the road to be straightened out. Except for pedestrian crossings, railings divide the road almost to the traffic lights at the foot of Lindum Hill. Lincoln Libraries now own the premises formerly used by Parke, White and Arnold, who closed in 1958. More demolition work was carried out on the east side of the Square to the north of the Royal British Legion premises, with the British Telecom Telephone Exchange, also set well back from the original building line, occupying a prominent position. Trees have been planted in front of the telephone exchange, further enhancing the now spacious aspect.

High Street and the Stonebow - in 1900. Lidgett's watchmakers, furniture dealers and auctioneers, had their premises on the corner of Saltergate and High Street. The Butter Market and the old Blue Boar Inn are discernible through the arch of the Stonebow.

Lidgett's shop was demolished in 1902 when Saltergate was widened. Pratt's, wine merchants, was rebuilt and left occupying the corner site. Almost opposite is the Old Original Silver Grill Restaurant. The motor car has probably just departed from the Saracen's Head Hotel.

Today, with the lower part of the building drastically altered, Richard Shops are on the corner of Saltergate and High Street and the area to the north and south of the 'Bow has been pedestrianised. The Saracen's Head closed in 1959 but the ornamental ironwork, formerly above the hotel entrance, has been retained.

Clasketgate, 1910. 'Big Wesley', or to give it its proper title, Wesley Methodist Chapel, was built in 1836 and demolished in 1963 to make way for a bank, shops and offices. During the Second World War the basement rooms were used as an annexe by the City School as the Army had requisitioned the temporary classrooms, affectionately known as 'The Huts' by both teaching staff and pupils, in what used to be Temple Street, Monks Road, now the College of Art and Technology.

The same view today, shops and a bank at street level, the offices above being used by British Telecom and an insurance company.

This view, immediately north of the Stonebow, was taken in 1915. Both Battle's, the chemist and Salter and Salter's boot stores were long established in what was then a most charming area of the city. Salter and Salter continued trading in the city until the mid 1930's and even today their advertisement can still be seen, albeit faintly, on the wall near to the old Midland level crossing. The Saracen's Head Hotel is visible through the Stonebow.

This typically modern - but controversial - structure replaced the old shops in 1971/72 and is in stark contrast to the 15th century gateway. It was a cause of great concern to many people in the city when the Saracen's Head was converted into shops in 1959.

Top of High Street looking south, circa 1920. Two familiar names are to be seen on the shop fronts in the immediate foreground. On left, Ruddocks, booksellers, printers and stationers since the 1880's and Bainbridge's, drapers, who started business about 30 years earlier.

Left

Today, Ruddock's remain a family business and still occupy the same spot. They also have a printing works elsewhere in the city. Bainbridge's stores were demolished and rebuilt in the 1920's and they are now part of a national concern. Their premises are at present occupied by Thom's.

Right

Bainbridge's, circa 1900. This photograph of Bainbridge's drapery department was probably taken about 1900 during the 'sales' early in the year, as indicated by the reduction in the price of all dresses. Compared with today, a vast contrast in selling practices is portrayed - note there are no less than six or seven soberly dressed assistants, resplendent in winged collars, silver watch-chains and pocket handkerchiefs. Notice also the comfort of the potential customer is duly considered by the provision of approximately ten chairs in the comparatively small sales room. Today, in many stores of this type, the staff would almost certainly be female and greatly reduced in number. The practice of providing chairs has also been discontinued in many emporia and even the playing of taped music in some establishments has, very often, to be endured, as has the hot and stuffy atmosphere.

DRESSES

Sibthorp House, an 18th century mansion situated on the east side of the High Street and near to the old Midland level crossing. It was built by the Sibthorp family, who later bought the Canwick Estate and lived at the hall.

The name's the same, but .... Sibthorp House was, unhappily, demolished in 1962 to make way for yet more shops and offices. Today, the only thing the old and the new buildings have in common is the retention of the name.

This is how the western end of St. Benedict Square looked at its junction with Brayford Head in the 1940's. Some property had already been demolished a few years earlier and the site used as a car park. The building with the archway, in centre of illustration, was shared by Clarke and Kinns, wholesale grocers, and G. Cliff and Sons, paper merchants, with the River Witham between the car park in the foreground and Brayford Wharf North. Just over Brayford Head Bridge can be seen the pub Royal William IV, with the premises of G. Harrison and Son, corn merchants, adjacent. Beyond Harrison's, the building, part of which overhangs the wharf, is Peel Bros., long established in the city, who were also corn merchants.

Today, this former peaceful scene on the waterfront has been drastically transformed by the construction of Wigford Way, which links High Street and Newland by way of a very busy dual carriageway affording easy access both to the west and the north. However, with the controversial removal of Brayford Head Bridge, traffic entering the city from the west and bound for the south of the industrial area of New Boultham, has been forced into High Street or across the city, whereas, if a bridge had been retained over Brayford Head, access to these areas would have been gained via Brayford Wharf East and Ropewalk, thus avoiding an already congested High Street. At the present time plans to alleviate this situation are under consideration by the Council. It will be seen that all the old property with the exception of the pub has completely disappeared with Sainsbury's new store in centre of picture and a multi-storey car park adjoining it. Automatic traffic signals are in operation at each end of Wigford Way and this is now one of the busiest roads in the city.

High Street, Looking north - 1920's. The two hotels situated on the east side of High Street no longer exist. The Spread Eagle Hotel was the first to go when Woolworth's acquired the premises in 1923 and the Saracen's Head shared a similar fate in 1959 when it, too, was converted into shops though the upper facade was retained. This lively scene was probably taken on a Saturday afternoon. It is interesting to see that, unlike today, almost everyone is wearing a hat of some description. The tower of the church of St. Peter-at-Arches can be seen to the right of the Stonebow.

Saturday afternoon again, with many shoppers thronging the High Street, but not a hat in sight! Littlewoods' stores now stand where the Regal Cinema and C.J. Fox's, drapers stood, until 1966. Opposite, although the Saracen's Head is no more, the wrought ironwork on the balcony has been retained. The towers to the right of the Stonebow in this illustration are the west towers of the Cathedral.